Hallelujah

Words and music by Leonard Cohen
Arranged for harp by Sylvia Woods

Performance Notes

Leonard Cohen's popular 1985 song *Hallelujah* has been recorded over 300 times. It gained a new generation of fans in 2001 when it was featured in the DreamWorks motion picture Shrek.

Leonard Cohen worked on this song for many years, and may have written over 80 draft verses. The verses included in this arrangement are the ones John Cale and Rufus Wainwright sang in Shrek. The lyrics for verses 1, 2, 3 and 5 are printed in the harp music. The full lyrics are printed on page 7.

I have arranged this piece for all levels of harp players. The first verse is easy, and each subsequent verse gets a bit more advanced. Beginners can play the first 1 or 2 verses, and more advanced players can continue on to the later verses. You may also repeat any verses that you'd like.

If you are stopping after one of the earlier verses, you'll want to end on a "C", to make the piece sound finished. So, in the last measure before the next verse starts, (the measure with the G chord), do not play what is written, just play a C note in the bass, and then stop.

As always, the fingerings in this music are only suggestions. There are a variety of ways to finger passages, particularly when there are repeated notes. Feel free to change any fingerings to suit your style.

Harp Ranges

The range needed for verses 1 to 3 are 20 strings, from a G up to an E. If you have a small harp with less than about 30 strings, you'll need to play the music an octave higher than written.

Verse 4 requires an extra octave, with 27 strings from G up to E. The very last note also goes down to a lower C, but this can be left out if necessary.

Hallelujah

Words and Music
by Leonard Cohen

Harp arrangement
by Sylvia Woods

I have arranged this piece for all levels of harp players. Each verse is a bit harder than the previous one. Beginners can play the first few verses, and more advanced players can continue on to the later verses. See the previous page for more information and suggestions.

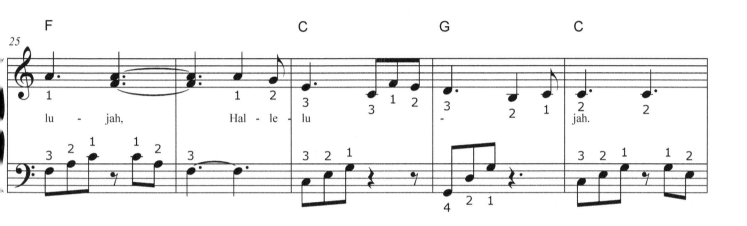

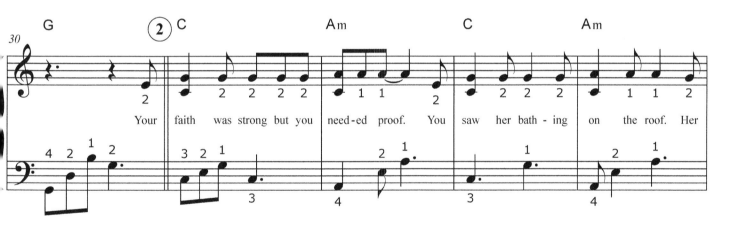

* this E may be left out for page turn

Lyrics

Verses 1, 2, 3, and 5 are printed in the music.

VERSE 1
I've heard there was a secret chord
That David played, and it pleased the Lord,
But you don't really care for music do you?
It goes like this: the fourth, the fifth,
The minor fall, the major lift,
The baffled king composing Hallelujah.

Hallelujah, Hallelujah, Hallelujah, Hallelujah.

VERSE 2
Your faith was strong but you needed proof.
You saw her bathing on the roof.
Her beauty and the moonlight overthrew you.
She tied you to a kitchen chair.
She broke your throne; and she cut your hair.
And from your lips she drew the Hallelujah.

VERSE 3
Maybe I've been here before.
I know this room; I've walked this floor.
I used to live alone before I knew you.
I've seen your flag on the marble arch.
Love is not a vict'ry march.
It's a cold and it's a broken Hallelujah.

VERSE 4 (not in this arrangement)
There was a time you let me know
What's real and going on below.
But now you never show it to me, do you?
And remember when I moved in you.
The holy dark was movin' too,
And every breath we drew was Hallelujah.

VERSE 5
Maybe there's a God above,
And all I ever learned from love
Was how to shoot at someone who outdrew you.
And it's not a cry you can hear at night.
It's not somebody who's seen the light.
It's a cold and it's a broken Hallelujah.

Hallelujah, Hallelujah, Hallelujah, Hallelujah.
Hallelujah, Hallelujah, Hallelujah, Hallelujah.